Reconcile

Reconcile

A Poetry Collection

Marie E. Lupinski

Hardcover ISBN: 979-8-9940467-3-9
Paperback ISBN: 979-8-9940467-1-5
Ebook ISBN: 979-8-9940467-2-2

Printed in the United States of America
First edition

"Life is what happens to you while you're busy making other plans"

— John Lennon

Introduction

For more than 55 years, I have had the joy and privilege of working with children, listening to their laughter, their questions and their boundless curiosity about the world. My career as a special educator has been filled with stories, lessons, and moments of wonder that have continued to shape who I am. Writing has always been another way for me to teach and to celebrate the beauty of words.

My children's book Grandma Across the Pond was born out of my love for language and the delightful differences between the way we speak English on either side of the Atlantic. It reminded me how words no matter where they come from can bridge oceans and generations.

This collection marks my first foray into poetry, a new chapter in my enduring relationship with words. Poetry allows me to explore feelings, memories, and the quiet moments that often go unnoticed. I hope to share glimpses of the world as I've seen it—as a teacher, a grandmother, and an ever-curious learner.

As a devoted student of Rumi, Sufi mystic and poet, I offer these reflections to you. May these verses inspire contemplation, spark joy, and remind readers of the extraordinary beauty woven into the everyday.

Poems

Song of Joining...13

Higher Place..15

Yes, It's True 16

Learning 19

Imbue 20

Connection..21

Reconcile...23

Seeing Who We Are...24

To Rumi 27

Trust 28

Answer..29

A Choice Distinctly Itself...30

Our Roots Run Deep 31

Breakdown of Denial..33

Go...35

Rotary 36

Beginning..38

Song Of Joining

The secret of divine life
Is a gift for all
Who share in the belief
That we are one

In our hesitation
To explore our union
We crumble our brains
Like food for birds

But that transfer of energy
Human and bird
Only solidifies truth
And our song of joining.

Higher Place

The turbulence of the ocean
Mimics the anger within
That knows not a clue of its beginning
But hopes for a peaceful end

As the moon regulates the tides
Let the pain be lifted to a higher place
Where anger becomes opportunity
And trust births answers.

Yes, It's True

I fall asleep in the chair

I give my heart and soul
To the work I do
Mending the psyches of children
Who are members of the forgotten few

The smiling face sometimes becoming an almost
Demonic energy
When pain is unbearable
The inner self sheds anger in order to cause synergy

The venom spews forth like an erupting volcano
Molten Lava hardening to form a new impenetrable heart
The cycle then begins again; it's almost time to start

I fall asleep in the chair

Coming home to the depressed you
Is another full-time job
My spirit gives you what is left
And then I feel robbed

The hours spent "Let's go here, let's go there"
All in an effort to allow
The light of day into your soul
Perhaps you will understand now

The worn threads of the sofa
Loosely woven where once they were tight
Staying awake to keep you company
Afraid to say goodnight

I fall asleep in the chair

What a wondrous thought that I have
In all our years together
The molehills became mountains
And forever became never

The giving bombarded me at first
My comfort zone attacked
It was no surprise to me
That I had to give it back

Was I worth the care and love?
I sent to you that message
And soon I was mother earth
And the relationship went into passage

If the only thing you can say to hurt
Is that I fell asleep in the chair
Then I must confess
I did my best
And that compliment is rare.

Learning

To open your heart
Does not mean to close your eyes
Allow every moment of life
To teach what is needed.

Imbue

Beautiful authentic self

Smiles at the travesty

Of what is real

Can she find beauty in authentic anger?

Will the authenticity trick her

Into thinking it could kill?

Kill the beautiful authentic self she once was

Before . . .

Before she started self-loathing

The beautiful authentic self

Beautiful authentic self

Looks in the mirror

And screams out in horror

When she realizes that beautiful authentic self

Has lost her image

And cannot reacquaint or reconnect

Or even recognize her beautiful authentic self

Crying out for self-acceptance.

Connection

A mother's love lives in shadows
There is no right or wrong
The soul spark ignited with birth
Connecting all knowledge
And what I used to remember
Time and clutter have allowed disconnection
It never lasts for long
And I feel again.

Reconcile

The tides change slowly
Fully experiencing the moon's power
It allows itself time for gratitude
Sometimes I want to tell these birds to shut up

Get away from me you are distracting
The words that need to flow from my mind
I'm trying to listen to the tide going out
And the interruption is rude

The birds and tides
Competing for my mind
When all I am looking for
Is a connection to soul

So much like the thoughts
That I want to ignore
They keep coming to visit
When quiet is desired.

Seeing Who We Are

We have traveled together

Into eternity

Our soul sparks igniting

Fires along the way

Once again we are a gift

In the divine existence of life

Our lessons to be learned

Need not create turmoil

Our lessons to be taught

Need not create pain

Infinite wisdom combines here

All intersections a must

Along the path of knowing

Comes that moment of recognition

When that person in the mirror is accepted

But, the you and me

Keep separate

The universal secret of union remains in the void

Until we accept our oneness.

To Rumi

I have had a rebirth
    Before I've actually lived
Words shared with me
    Have been spoken many centuries ago
Yet, they speak to me now in a loud voice

The metamorphosis of divine love
    And understanding
Transcends all time
    And offers an invitation

To reconnect to all that was
    Is
And all that will be.

Trust

You want to serve and give more
 But there's no one to accept
You know your life's purpose
 But there's nowhere it's understood
Speak the language of life to the universe
 Let it really hear you
 Like you have never allowed before
 Scream it out of your heart
Unlock the emotion of the soul
 Don't keep it under such tight security
 No one wants to hurt you
 And you'll only know that if you trust
Trust yourself to know
That when you share your innermost thoughts
You will only choose to tell
Those who will honor
Destiny is a funny thing
 It's not all that serious and dark
 Perhaps the light you need to live
 Can be turned on by another.

Answer

When I want to connect
I close my eyes
And go within
To that special place
Where there is no question
Only the answer to why I exist.

A Choice Distinctly Itself

Matters of the heart are sometimes gray

Black or white the villains of love

Gray the provider of balance

White with a little black

Could that be gray?

Black with a lot of white

Mimics gray too

Gray is a place, a feeling

And always a choice distinctly itself

It tickles the light

And laughs at the dark

Yet gray spiritually recognizes the fact

That compromise and love are next-door neighbors

And the white picket fence

Sometimes falls into the black night

Preventing sunshine from living in our hearts

Forever.

Our Roots Run Deep

The tree cries out for love
As it shrivels and dies
My tears give it that one final impulse
To try and live a bit longer
But that tree and I
Have no separate life
And cannot collude a path
We travel together into infinity
Where all that was is . . .

Breakdown Of Denial

The quiet of the noise

Comforts my ears

The silence of not hearing

Overshadows my emotion

Hears the quiet

Go within

The privilege of seeing and hearing

Is yours

Learn from the pain

What it is that hurts

And face the light

Within yourself . . .

Go

I want you to be happy

On your desired path

But you, far away causes pain

This is my brain talking

Not my heart

It knows

We live together.

You see

I hear

You feel

I cry

The union of all is understood.

Rotary

Don't you ask questions
When you come to a rotary?

One mile of extra traffic
Or a gift of time

One more mile of extra traffic
Or a gift of some good songs

One more mile of extra traffic
Or a gift of good conversation

There are no accidents
And time slots open and close each moment

One more mile of traffic
Or a gift of life

Don't ask questions
When you come to a rotary

The circle of life begins and ends

With the universal decision to move forward without fear.

Beginning

The end
Is just the beginning
Of what we know
As eternity.

Endorsements

Marie's poetry melds the normalcy of life with profound insights. Reconcile is an adventure of the mind and soul where life's smallest moments become windows into understanding ourselves and others.
Maria Massei-Rosato

A powerful but gentle tapestry of everyday emotions and sensations we often leave untapped.
Paula Grudko

Writes with the spirit of Rumi words that dance between heaven and heart. Her poetry is a lantern for the soul, illuminating love, longing and the quiet grace within us all.
Pam Schaneen

It has taken a few readings of the full body of your poetry to discern the essence . . . A longing, a deep yearning for genuine self-acceptance in the midst of full offering of self—both light and dark sides—to another, to yourself, to life . . . only . . . to lose the connection TO SELF again . . . and again . . . and yet again . . . never fully arriving safely home.
Linda Smith

Each poem shimmers with honesty and grace—a remarkable debut from a singular talent.
Johanna Pawlo

Acknowledgment

I would like to acknowledge my granddaughter, Charlotte, who has taught me through her poetry to be brave.

About the Author

A lifelong educator, Marie Lupinski created the David Gregory School for children on the Autism spectrum, 33 years ago.